Lynn Lyons Morris
Carol Taylor Fitz-Gibbon

Center for the Study of Evaluation
University of California, Los Angeles

SAGE PUBLICATIONS Beverly Hills/London

For information address:

Sage Publications, Inc.
275 South Beverly Drive
Beverly Hills, California 90212

Sage Publications Ltd
28 Banner Street
London EC1Y 8QE

Printed in the United States of America

International Standard Book Number 0-8039-1065-7
Library of Congress Catalog Card No. 78-57012

TWELFTH PRINTING, 1986

Table of Contents

Acknowledgements

This book is part of the *Program Evaluation Kit.* The kit contains eight books, each covering a topic commonly confronted by evaluators of educational programs. The kit was developed over a four year period as a project of the Center for the Study of Evaluation (CSE), University of California, Los Angeles, funded by the National Institute of Education. Many people besides the kit's authors contributed to its eventual publication either conceptually or through technical support.

The idea of writing such a kit we owe to Dr. Marvin C. Alkin, Director of CSE from 1968 to 1975. Dr. Eva L. Baker, current Center Director, provided the continuing solid support and lively interest necessary for its completion. Dr. Adrianne Bank, first as co-director of the kit project in its early stages and finally in her role as the Center's Associate Director, gave us the moral support necessary to traverse the arduous final stages of kit production.

Several staff members aided in the kit's extensive field test–151 sites throughout the United States and Canada. We thank Margeret Dotseth, Richards Smith Williams, and Esther Goldstein for their painstaking work in gathering and organizing field test data.

Kit booklets were extensively reviewed by experts in the areas of evaluation research, methodology, and measurement. Comments on the content of sections of this book were made by Dr. Jason Millman, Cornell University; Dr. Ernest House, University of Illinois; and Dr. Fred Niedermeyer, Southwest Regional Laboratory. These reviewers not only made valuable suggestions for revision of early drafts, but by either using the materials in classes with students or by discussing translation of technical issues into lay language, they gave the authors a strong sense of the kit's usefulness as both a procedural guide and educational tool.

The authors wish to thank members of the Center's technical support staff who worked hard to keep manageable the production of such a large work. Donna Anderson Cuvelier carried the major responsibility for typing, organizing, and supervising manuscript preparation. Ruth Paysen ably shouldered part of the burden of typing the extensive manuscript.

Gracious thanks are also in order to Mr. Lou Orsan who provided advice about graphic design in the preparation of the field test draft of the kit and who designed the books finally published.

Significant editorial and conceptual work was done on this particular book by Mr. Michael Bastone to whom the authors own a great debt of thanks.

We wish finally to thank Ms. Cheryl Tyler of the UCLA Office of Contracts and Grants who ably ushered the kit through final legal channels toward publication.

Lynn Lyons Morris

Carol Taylor Fitz-Gibbon

Los Angeles, California
August 1978

Introduction

Educational programs are intended to achieve goals. The goals may be general, such as greater communication skills, or specific, such as correct use of words from a certain vocabulary list. They may deal solely with the educational setting and be realized relatively quickly, such as compliance with desegregation requirements; or they may aim at long-range outcomes of learning experiences, such as harmony among members of different racial groups.

Education seeks to *accomplish* its goals by means of *programs* initiated within a school or district setting. Usually some organizational change occurs, or teachers interact with students using the curricular activities and materials which the program prescribes.

Two major questions are addressed during the evaluation of educational programs:

- To what degree were *goals* attained?
- What actually *took place* when the program was carried out?[1]

1. A comprehensive discussion of methods for detecting and describing the means and processes that comprise an educational program is found in the booklet, *How to Measure Program Implementation,* part of the *Program Evaluation Kit.*

Clear delineation of program goals is the first component of a good evaluation, and is the central concern of this book. More specifically, the booklet is designed to help you accomplish major program evaluation tasks related to goals and objectives. It will:

- Demonstrate the need for writing clearly defined statements of goals, outcomes, and objectives
- Provide direction and examples for writing these statements
- Provide a method for deriving goals and objectives from already published materials
- Demonstrate the relationship between writing objectives and constructing test items
- Outline methods for measuring the attainment of a large number of objectives when testing time is limited

The booklet should help you develop some basic skills in dealing with goals and objectives for the purpose of planning an evaluation. Its contents are based on the experience of evaluators at the Center for the Study of Evaluation, University of California, Los Angeles, and on the field-test experiences of people in school settings who used an earlier edition.

Wherever possible, the booklet recommends procedures, rules of thumb, and practical strategies for performing evaluation tasks related to goals and objectives.[2] Keep in mind that many of the recommended procedures are methods for working with objectives under advantageous circumstances. Few evaluation situations, of course, exactly match the situations envisioned here, so *you should not expect to be able to duplicate the suggestions in the booklet.* It is hoped that you will examine the

2. In discussing the development and use of objectives, little effort has been made to distinguish affective objectives from ability objectives since most of the principles and procedures discussed apply to objectives in general.

principles and examples provided, and adapt them to the press of your own time constraints and data requirements.

Evaluation is a new field. Few procedures for accomplishing evaluation are hard and fast. The task of any evaluator is to provide information to program funders, staff, and others with a stake in program processes and outcomes. Your obligation, therefore, is to gather the most highly credible information possible within the constraints of your situation, and to present your conclusions to each evaluation audience in a form that makes the information useful to them.

The *Program Evaluation Kit,* of which this booklet is one component, is intended for use primarily by people who have been assigned the role of *program evaluator.* Your job as an evaluator takes one of two shapes, depending on the task you have been assigned:

1. You may have responsibility for producing a *summary statement* about the effectiveness of the program. In this case, you probably will report to a funding agency or governmental group representing the program's constituency. You may be expected to describe the program, to produce a statement concerning the program's achievement of announced goals, to note any unanticipated outcomes, and possibly to make comparisons with alternative programs. If these are the features of your job, you are a *summative evaluator.*
2. Your evaluation task may characterize you as a *helper* and *advisor* to the program planners and developers. You may then be called on to look out for potential problems, identify areas where the program needs improvement, describe and monitor program activities, and periodically test for progress in achievement or attitude change. In this situation, you are a "jack of all trades," a person whose overall task is not well defined. You may or may not be required to produce a report at the end of your activities. If this more loosely defined job role seems closer to yours, then you are a *formative evaluator.*

Most of the information regarding goals and objectives contained in this booklet will be useful for both formative and summative tasks. Your perspective on the statement of goals and objectives may vary somewhat, depending on which of the two roles is yours, but both evaluation roles carry the responsibility of keeping the program true to its announced purposes. Also, in both situations it is common to find that the program planners have failed to provide statements of goals and objectives that are specified well enough to help you carry out that responsibility.

The summative evaluator will be primarily interested in finding and using instruments to measure attainment of the goals of the program. This calls for goal statements that can serve as a basis for constructing or purchasing measures of the program's major desired outcomes.

The formative evaluator will have diverse uses for goals and objectives. In order to make it possible for both the staff and the evaluator to agree about the basis on which the program will be evaluated, goals will need to be clearly stated and written down, and it is up to the evaluator to elicit and develop such statements in conjunction with the program planners. In addition, the formative evaluator will want to design at least informal measures to make progress checks and to use with short experiments. Well conceived instruments measuring enroute objectives can, in turn, influence the content of the tests that will be needed for the summative evaluation of the program. Thus, the formative evaluator is interested in general goal statements that will encourage dialogue about the program, as well as in minute, behavioral goal statements that can be used for designing instruments to measure program progress or overall impact.

Formative evaluators will have some influence over curricular decisions and changes in the program, so they may be interested in the section of the booklet dealing with how to derive objectives from standardized tests. On the other hand, the section that discusses the use of standardized tests to evaluate programs may be of greater interest to summative evaluators. Both formative and summative evaluators may find it necessary to better focus the evaluation by reducing the number of objectives, as described in Chapter 4. While the summative evaluator might use any of the methods discussed, the formative evaluator is most likely to use ratings or hierarchies to prioritize objectives.

In most cases, it is good practice to seek out already written goals and objectives, since writing goal statements, whether for curriculum development or for evaluation, is a difficult and time-consuming task. The chapters on locating and writing goals and objectives may also be useful to you if you are preparing to write a proposal.

Whatever your reasons for reading this booklet, it is presented as an introduction to the issues and tasks surrounding goal setting and preferencing in evaluation. You will find suggestions for further reading at the end of most chapters so that you may explore in greater depth those topics that particularly interest you.

Chapter 1

Goals and Objectives in Evaluation

We human beings are special, say the philosophers, partly because we visualize things as they could be, and not just as they are now. Writers in the field of education have given much thought to how things could be or should be in the world, and they look to education as the means by which people may become:

- Good, responsible citizens
- Creative, self-fulfilled individuals
- Altruistic participants in a free democracy
- Flexible thinkers

Notwithstanding the importance of such lofty visions, it is equally important to confront people and conditions as they are *now*. As someone involved with the schools, you function in a day-to-day situation in which the realization of great aims depends on practical, real-life planning and action. Very likely, you have at some time set up an in-service workshop or have had long heart-to-heart talks with a distressed teacher or an unhappy parent precisely because you have *goals* in mind for the teachers, the parents, and the students. Your goals, of course, are apt to be more limited and concrete than the goals mentioned above.

In the same way, a new program (like the one you are evaluating now) comes into existence because a particular teacher, or some concerned group, like a committee of administrators, parents, and teachers, has in mind a set of goals that the program is intended to accomplish. This set of goals, once you start to examine it closely, is probably quite large, and could range from the grand, approximating those mentioned above, to the most mundane, for example, reducing the number of students using the restroom at one time. In addition, unless a formal program plan or proposal has been written, it is likely that no one has spent time spelling out all the goals toward which the program is aimed. It is a fair assumption that some goals, buried in the values system of your community, have not yet been made clear.

Your first task as evaluator will be to develop a list of goals or objectives that explains without ambiguity what the planners of the program agree it should accomplish[3]—be they parents, teachers, a committee, or you alone. This must be done for three reasons:

1. A major benefit from performing an evaluation is the dialogue that results from making the goals and activities of the program known to interested groups. Evaluation encourages teachers and program planners to discuss openly their intentions for the program—what they believe it can realistically accomplish. Evaluation is also a vehicle for carrying information about the program to the general public. If a community-wide needs assessment accompanies the evaluation, parents and concerned citizens can be given a chance to voice their preferences about school goals. Even in the absence of a needs assessment, an evaluation tends to focus community attention on a program, thus opening its intended outcomes to scrutiny. An evaluation can trigger this healthy interchange of ideas whether it is summative, and therefore intended to focus on program *accountability,* or formative, helping with *improvement* of a new or ongoing program.

   Often, you may find that when an implicit goal is translated into clear statement of a concrete outcome, the result may not please certain groups or staff members. The process of resolving these differences might be painful, but it provides everyone involved with the opportunity to develop a more precise notion of what the program is about.

2. People responsible for funding or public opinion will *judge* the program (i.e., evaluate it) in terms of how well it accomplishes worthwhile goals. There are evaluation theorists, in fact, who consider the bedrock of an evaluation to be the precise delineation of goals. Furthermore, when it

3. The chapter "How to Play the Role of Formative Evaluator," part of the *Evaluator's Handbook, Program Evaluation Kit,* describes methods for helping groups agree about their objectives.

comes time to collect data to determine how well your program accomplished its goals, your choice of what data to collect will be based on the clear statement of your goals.

3. Some of the best evaluations *compare* the findings from one program with the results from another. Such comparisons are particularly useful when both programs can be shown to be teaching toward the same goals.

Thus, in evaluation, goals form a basis for discussion of the program, and for measurement and data collection. They provide, as well, the foundation for comparison of competing programs.

Some Advice About Stating Goals

Goals must be stated specifically so that the public can tell whether they have been achieved. Whatever words you use in writing your goals, at some point you will want a statement that is clear enough to provide a yardstick for measuring program success. Clear goals stated in concrete terms are usually referred to as objectives. The critical need for clarity in stating goals and objectives has led educators to evolve directives about how to do this. These directives are discussed at length throughout the booklet.

Be careful to keep separate the goals you define which describe outcomes, that is, measurable end products of the program, and those that define processes, that is, the means for accomplishing them. The major focus of most evaluations is on the accomplishment of outcome objectives (ends-goals). A method for discriminating ends-goals from means-goals is to subject them to a simple test:

- *Ends-goals* should describe abilities or attitudes that complete the sentence, "At the end of the program, the students–or parents, or teachers–will demonstrate. . . ."
- *Means-goals* will fit this sentence: "During the program, students–or parents, or teachers–will take part in. . . ."

This booklet, like most treatments of the role of goals and objectives in evaluation, focusses on the use of ends-goals.

It is important to note, however, that in most circumstances, you will want to pay attention to means-goals as well. You may even decide to build the evaluation solely around means-goals. This will focus the evaluation upon determining whether particular instructional activities have occurred, disregarding the outcome of these activities. The evaluation audience may desire, for instance, to ensure that individualized instruction is taking place in a junior high, rather than to monitor the effects of this particular process on achievement. Also, when there are special difficulties associated with measuring the *affective or attitude outcomes* of your program, you may opt to measure related factors such as student attention and participation *during* class sessions. For some remote or ephemeral goals, such as responsible adulthood, good citizenship, or self-directed learning, you *will not be able* to measure outcomes. In such instances, you should measure the extent of implementation of activities which, from someone's point of view at least, *are likely to bring about* these remote outcomes. In any of these cases, if the evaluation audience is willing, it will be legitimate to base your evaluation upon means-goals stated in terms of program activities.

Then, too, the *means* your program uses (materials, activities, and the like) are certainly important to the program. In fact, they are the program, and any evaluation should pay attention to describing them.

When you state means-goals as part of your evaluation, use the "During the program . . ." stem described here. Special methods, usually described as "implementation measures," are available for measuring use of program activities and materials.[4] This component of the evaluation should appear separate from discussion of outcomes in the *Program Implementation* section of your evaluation report.

If you intend to conduct an evaluation focussed on ends-goals that compares the outcomes of two competing programs, the ends-goals that are common to both will form your basis for comparison. There will probably be additional goals for each program that are not alike. Their difference presents no problem to your evaluation as long as the goals shared by both are ones that you consider fairly important.

The term "goals" usually refers to general statements about where an educational program is headed. It is important that a goal statement meet the three previously mentioned conditions:

1. Its meaning should be clear to the people involved.
2. It should be agreed upon by the program planners and funders.
3. It should be clearly identifiable as dealing with either ends or means.

In addition:

---

4. See *How to Measure Program Implementation,* part of the *Program Evaluation Kit.*

4. It should be realistic in terms of time and money available for achieving it.

If these four conditions are met, then goal statements to guide planning or discussion may be stated even as generally as the following:

- To increase attendance at school athletic events
- We want students genuinely to enjoy school
- They should learn to cooperate with others
- Better achievement-test results
- Fluent French
- The child will develop an understanding of mathematical principles

If you prefer, you may express your goals in the form of *evaluation questions.* In some cases, couching the goal in question-form encourages those involved to begin thinking about ways of demonstrating goal achievement. The above goals stated in the question format become:

- Has attendance at school athletic activities increased?
- Are our students enjoying school more now?
- Have our students learned to cooperate better with others?
- Are achievement test results better now than before the program?
- Are students fluent in French?
- Have the children developed an understanding of mathematical principles?

General goals of the sort described here are helpful for many evaluation and planning purposes, for instance, communicating the intent of a curriculum development effort. For actually evaluating a program's specific achievements, however, they may be too vague. As evaluator, you will often need to design ways of *measuring* goal attainment. Goals this general suggest too many potential measures. Consider, for instance, the thousand ways you could assess "fluent French." For the sake of focussing the evaluation, someone—probably you—will have to hone such goals into more finely tuned objectives.

Outcome objectives (usually called behavioral, or performance, or instructional objectives) describe the *behavior* that the program's target group should evidence at its conclusion as proof that they learned something. As such, objectives describe, or strongly suggest, the sort of test that should evaluate the program.[5]

The following example may clarify the relationship among broad goals, subsidiary goals, and behavioral objectives.

A broad goal in language arts might be:

The student will develop grammatical skills in writing.

A more specific subsidiary goal might be:

The student will understand and apply basic rules of usage and agreement.

A behavioral objective within the scope of the subsidiary goal might be:

Given a simple sentence (one subject, one predicate), the student will write "OK" if the subject agrees in number with the verb and, if not, will write a form of the same verb that would correctly revise the sentence.

A broad goal itself cannot be measured by a test. Nevertheless, behaviors associated with it can be measured by a test assessing its myriad subsidiary objectives. Broad and specific goals provide a general direction for planning, but only behavioral objectives can be measured. The measurement of these objectives provides fundamental evidence for the evaluation.

Some Background on Behavioral Objectives

The field of evaluation was the spawning ground and birthplace of the by-now sophisticated and famous Behavioral Objective. Behavioral objectives are announcements of desired program outcomes that are stated as behaviors. While behavioral objectives are now used (and abused) for many purposes, they were originally intended as guides for accumulating evidence that educational goals had been met.

5. *Process* objectives similarly describe the behaviors and activities in which program participants should engage. These form a basis for measuring program implementation. Process objectives and assessment of implementation, while beyond the scope of this book, are addressed in *How to Measure Program Implementation*, another booklet in the *Program Evaluation Kit*.

A behavioral objective is a statement of certain behaviors that, if exhibited by students, indicate that the students have some skill, attitude, or knowledge.

This is reasonable enough when you consider that all we can see of students' achievement in our program is what they show us–how they behave. No matter how complex or subtle the knowledge or attitudes to be taught by the program that you are evaluating, you must look to student performance for *evidence* of learning. The behavioral objectives of a program list those critical performances that you, or the staff, or the evaluation audience will accept as evidence that the students (or parents, or teachers–whoever is the program's target) have learned something or acquired an attitude.

You might like to think of your evaluation in this way: Knowledge of a specific topic–say the American Civil War–could be considered analogous to a gigantic iceberg, with the great substructure underwater, and unobservable, and the tip sticking out above. For centuries, ocean navigators have needed to see no more than a small peak above the water, and they've known what's down there! Navigators don't have to carefully examine every detail of the submerged iceberg–its density or volume. They look at the size and character of what's on top, and they know enough to stay away.

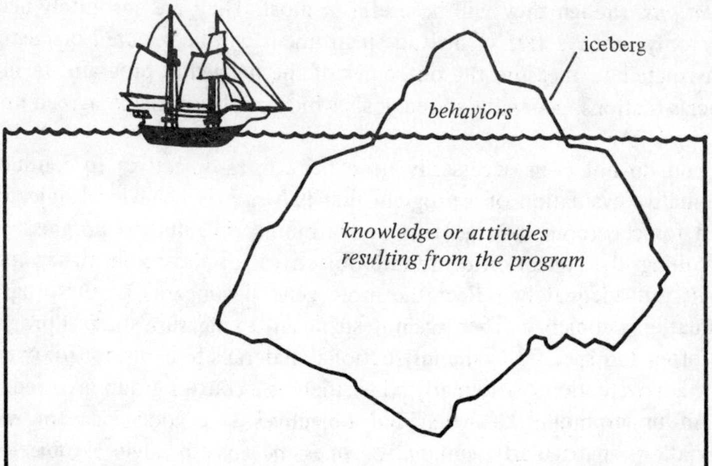

Similarly, a carefully thought-out behavioral objective (or more usually, a set of them) defines an observable indication that the evaluator takes as a sign that the knowledge (or attitude or skill) is *in there.* A set of three behavioral objectives designed to measure whether sixth graders have gained a basic understanding of the Civil War period might be:

> Asked to list two economic and four political differences underlying the North/South rivalry that triggered the Civil War, the student will do so.
>
> Given a set of names of Civil War battles, the student will write a paragraph about the significance of the battle in furthering the North or South's campaign.
>
> Asked to sing at least two period songs and recite at least two popular legends surrounding the Civil War, the student will do so.

Certainly these behavioral objectives do not exhaust all there is to know about the Civil War. Rather, some person or group has surveyed the possibilities and decided that these behaviors satisfactorily represent the broad knowledge-base concerning the Civil War that is the goal of *their* American History program.

Thus, behavioral objectives define behaviors which indicate the students have the competency, skill, or attitude which the behavior reflects.

Precisely stated behavioral objectives are not necessary in all evaluation situations, though they will be useful in most. They are absolutely necessary only when a test or attitude instrument will be selected or custom-constructed to measure the outcomes of the particular program. In most other situations, generally stated goals which can be mutually agreed upon will probably suffice.

You do not even necessarily need behavioral objectives to conduct a summative evaluation of a program that is *based on* behavioral objectives used for classroom management or for monitoring student progress. For one thing, the collection of minute objectives for classroom management might not adequately reflect the more general concerns of the program evaluation's audience. Then again, tests meant to measure student progress are often too specific to the instructional materials to be useful for overall program evaluation, particularly when there is a control group involved.

An underpinning of behavioral objectives is a good idea for most evaluations—particularly summative ones—because behavioral objectives clearly suggest the content of a *test.* And construction of a test custom-fitted to the overall objectives of the program to be evaluated is the most sensitive means for detecting program effects. A test based on the program's own objectives or on the combined objectives of two competing programs should provide an excellent measure of how well the program has done. Conversely, standardized tests like those given at the end of the year in most school districts may constitute a poor measure (see the section in this booklet, pp. 43 to 46, entitled, "Using a Standardized Test To Evaluate a Program"). It is particularly desirable to create your own test in situations where you find that you must use a before-and-after design (that is, a design without a comparison group) to assess program results. Since the before-and-after design usually lacks comparison criteria for determining the actual worth of apparently good results, a thorough description of the program and its intended outcomes will make your evaluation more convincing. A good and currently popular way to ensure a credible evaluation of a program is to build the evaluation around behavioral objectives commonly agreed upon by the program staff. *Showing that a program meets certain specific absolute standards* (such as having children read basic words in first grade) provides genuinely crucial information about its effectiveness—even in the absence of a comparison group.

Whether you choose to organize the evaluation according to general goal statements or specific behavioral objectives, you will save yourself time and effort if you locate *already written* goals and objectives and adapt them where necessary, rather than attempt to write myriad ones yourself. The next chapter attempts to help you find goals and objectives collections relevant to your situation. In Chapter 3, the section entitled, "How to Write Behavioral Objectives," will help you to write precise behavioral objectives in the event that you wish to use them.

For Further Reading

Gorth, W. P., O'Reilly, R. P., & Pinsky, P. D. *Comprehensive achievement monitoring: A criterion referenced evaluation system.* Englewood Cliffs, NJ: Educational Technology Publications, 1975.

Kapfer, M. B., Ed. *Behavioral objectives in curriculum development: Selected readings and bibliography.* Englewood Cliffs, NJ: Educational Technology Publications, 1971.

Krathwohl, D. R., & Payne, D. A. The nature and definition of educational objectives and strategies for their assessment. In R. L. Thorndike (Ed.), *Educational measurement* (2nd ed.). Washington, D.C.: American Council on Education, 1971.

Mager, R. F. *Preparing instructional objectives* (2nd ed.). Belmont, CA: Fearon Publishers, 1962.

Chapter 2

Where to Find Goals and Objectives

In some situations, an evaluator might be asked to evaluate a program for which no clear statement of objectives has been made, but for which objectives are needed. The best solution to this problem lies with the program staff: Have them write objectives against which they think the program should be evaluated. You, as evaluator, will likely have to review these objectives and, if necessary, put them into behavioral form.

Sometimes, the job of defining objectives will fall upon the evaluator. Generally, this occurs when it is assumed that the evaluator possesses some expertise or general information about the type of program being evaluated. Whether you or someone else is given responsibility for developing objectives, you should consult some of the following sources to ensure that your list is representative of what the program's objectives ought to be:

- State or federal mandates and legislation
- Local and national concerns identified in editorials, articles, and legislation
- Parental concerns as voiced in letters, PTA and parent advisory meetings, and conferences with parents
- Community concerns voiced by business organizations, pressure groups, and the like
- School records and reports, such as attendance, discipline, career choices of graduates, and test scores
- College requirements and employers' requirements for graduates.

- Teacher reports and comments
- Student requests and comments
- Project proposals, final evaluation reports, and program descriptions of other projects in the same curriculum area
- Other schools which have developed programs in your area of interest

You may also want to consult lists of educational goals and objectives that have been collected and published in various forms. The sources given below are not exhaustive, but do cover a wide range of grade levels and subject matter. They give a fair indication of what is currently (1978) available in the United States to the educator who wishes to select from existing collections of educational goals and objectives. There are, at present, few sources of measurable-objectives collections in the *affective* domain, although some objectives dealing with attitudes in various school subjects are frequently included in collections of cognitive objectives in those subjects. Some attitude objectives that are not tied to particular subjects are available from the Institute for Educational Research and the Instructional Objectives Exchange (listed below), but are presented in conjunction with those publishers' particular test items or inventories. In addition, you will find some affective objectives in the CSE Test Evaluation series developed at the Center for the Study of Evaluation.

Sources of Measurable Objectives in a Variety of Subject Areas

Clark County Curriculum Guides	available from: Clark County School District 2832 East Flamingo Road Las Vegas, Nevada 89121
Course Goals Developed by the Tri-County Project	available from: Commercial-Educational Distributing Services P.O. Box 8723 Portland, Oregon 97208

Elective Quarter Plan Curriculum Materials, Grades 1-12	available from: Director of Curriculum Jefferson County Board of Education 3023 Melbourne Avenue Louisville, Kentucky 40220
Evaluation for Individualized Instruction (EII) Pool of Behavioral Objectives and Test Items for K-12 in Language Arts, Math, Social Science, and Science	available from: Institute for Educational Research 1400 West Maple Avenue Downers Grove, Illinois 60515
Individual Pupil Monitoring System (IPMS) Behavioral Objectives Booklets for Grades 1-6 in Reading and Grades 1-8 in Mathematics	available from: The Test Dept., Houghton-Mifflin Company 777 California Avenue Palo Alto, California 94304
Learning Objectives and Behavioral Objectives (Primary, Secondary, Junior College)	available from: Cambridge Book Company 488 Madison Avenue New York, New York 10022
Measurable Objectives Collection in Many Subjects for Grades K-12	available from: Instructional Objectives Exchange Box 24095 Los Angeles, California 90024
Objectives and Items for K-12 in Language Arts, Math, Social Science, Science, and Vocational Education	available from: The Co-op 413 Hills House North University of Massachusetts Amherst, Massachusetts 01002
Specimen Set of *Mastery; an Evaluation Tool* for Reading and Math, Grades K-9	available from: Science Research Associates, Inc. 259 East Erie Street Chicago, Illinois 60611

Sources of Broadly-Stated Goals and Goal Categories

Brochures of Objectives in Art, Career and Occupational Development, Literature, Mathematics, Music Reading, Science, Social Studies, and Writing	available from: National Assessment of Educational Progess 700 Lincoln Tower 1860 Lincoln Street Denver, Colorado 80203
Taxonomy of Educational Objectives, Handbooks I & II	available from: David McKay Co., Inc. 750 Third Avenue New York, New York 10017
Workshop Packet for Educational Goals and Objectives	available from: Phi Delta Kappa, Inc. Eighth Street & Union Avenue Box 789 Bloomington, Indiana 47401

Additional sets of objectives are often found accompanying items on criterion-referenced tests. In some cases, program objectives may also be derived from the standardized tests that will be used for program evaluation. The use of standardized, norm-referenced tests as a basis for developing objectives is discussed in the next chapter.

Chapter 3

Writing Your Own Objectives

How to Write Behavioral Objectives

Behavioral objectives are so named because they are the offspring of the school of behaviorism in psychology. The behaviorists investigated the *responses* humans learned to make in the presence of *stimuli,* and tried to discover rules governing the stimulus-response relationship. Behaviorism's major paradigm, probably familiar to you, was

$$S \longrightarrow R$$

Stimulus causes response.

To the behaviorist, *learning* was the establishment of this connection, and observed behavior the only true source of data.

In education, the stimulus-response paradigm was translated into the behavioral objective, and though behaviorism itself proved unequal to the task of explaining the complexity of human cognition, the behavioral objective remains a useful tool for the educational evaluator.[6] The reason for this is quite simple in its logic. Much of the evaluation depends on the development of tests; tests become the *stimuli* to which students who have learned something make a *response.* In other words, the human mind may be vastly complex, but the world of testing is without doubt one of stimulus and response.

---

6. Some educators, hoping to throw off association with a somewhat mechanistic psychological school-of-thought, have turned to the terms "performance" or "instructional" objectives. However named, the essential nature of such objectives remains unchanged.

This bit of history is intended to help you understand the reasoning process which underlies the writing of behavioral objectives for your evaluation. Every behavioral objective anticipates the statement of a test stimulus and its intended reaction, namely the correct response that will be made by a student who has the desired skill or attitude. The behavioral objective provides the basis for the test that will be given to check whether a goal (outcome, end) has been reached.

The following format, or some paraphrase of it, should be adequate for every outcome objective you write, no matter what the area of learning:

GIVEN ______ (here you name the stimulus) ______

THE STUDENT WILL ______ (here you name the desired response) ______

Filling in these blanks with appropriate stimuli and responses will yield behavioral objectives. For example:

GIVEN *6 pieces of red, 6 of white, and 6 of blue cloth in disarray,* THE STUDENT WILL *sort them into three piles on the basis of color.*

GIVEN *the formula* $X = V_1 t + \frac{1}{2}gt^2$, THE STUDENT WILL *write a problem to which the formula is applicable as a solution.*

GIVEN *6 written paragraphs,* THE STUDENT WILL *identify their main ideas.*

Filling in blanks is not all there is to it, of course. There are a few important principles to keep in mind when you write down a program's objectives:

Principle No. 1: Behavioral objectives are used only for describing ends intended by the program, not means

Unfortunately, this principle is easy to forget. Even in a list of the most professionally developed objectives, you may find one or two mistaken inclusions that talk about program activities. Consider the following:

Given a lesson explaining the six simple machines, the teacher will present it so that the students have a chance to discover mechanical principles.

Given a reading-teaching machine, the student will use it 15 minutes every day.

In the first example, good practice is violated by the error of specifying a response that is to be made *by the teacher.* Unless the objective is part of a teacher-training program–in which case the teacher is the student–specifying teacher behavior is not allowed in posing the objective. Remember that what the teacher does is part of the *means* of instruction.

In the second example, the objective contains a more common error, more difficult to detect. It describes student behavior, but it does not describe the desired *outcome/end* behavior. Rather, if you read it carefully, you will note that it prescribes a *means* by which students will gain a skill. No doubt the writer of the objective expected an outcome that could be specified as a behavior showing some improvement in reading. As written, however, the statement confuses means and ends. A corrected version of this same objective might be:

> Given the posttest for the first unit of instruction on the reading-teaching machine, the student will obtain a passing score.

It is, of course, proper that the writer should want the students to engage in certain learning activities. But there is no reason to phrase learning activities–means–as behavioral objectives. A behavioral objective, since it is a first step toward writing a test, must point to the end product of learning. The means for reaching this end product will be an entirely separate concern. Since this is the case, it is well to take the time, after writing a set of behavioral objectives for a program, to ask yourself about each objective: Is this an end that I desire and for which I intend to test, or is it a means to that end?

Principle No. 2: The objectives for a program should reflect the different levels of skill attainment it intends to produce

How you phrase an objective reflects the extent to which you intend the student to have mastered an area of subject matter or the depth to which you expect an attitude to be assumed. A science program, for instance, can be aimed, at its least ambitious level, toward student mastery of basic concepts:

> . . . the student will write definitions of terms describing the major parts of a flower.

Then again, if the curriculum aims toward more complex skills, the science program might want to produce deeper understanding:

. . . the student will write an essay describing the role of the various parts of a flower in ensuring reproduction.

The program might even seek to develop quite advanced abilities:

. . . the student will invent an adequate system for classifying the dicotyledons according to the structure of their flower parts.

Most programs seek to develop some skills and attitudes at several levels of attainment. Often, however, their accompanying objectives do not adequately reflect this range; they concentrate heavily on lower-level memory skills.

As you develop or review the objectives for a program, bear in mind the need to have the pool of a program's objectives adequately reflect its range. The best way to help yourself to include objectives at varied complexity levels is to consult the taxonomies of educational objectives written by Bloom and others for cognitive skills and by Krathwohl and others for the attainment of attitudes and values. The publications that describe these taxonomies include illustrative educational objectives and test items. Tables 1 and 2 present an outline of the taxonomies.

If you are adequately familiar with the program being evaluated, look through the appropriate taxonomy and ask yourself which higher-level skills the program aims to teach. If your knowledge of the program contents is limited, then ask its planners or staff to help you *ensure that its objectives match the range and depth of its content.* The following are examples of some questions to keep in mind:

- Does the program seek to encourage comprehension and application of basic principles?
- Does it seek to teach students skills involving critical thinking, evaluation, or creativity ("synthesis")?
- Does the program aim to develop tolerance ("receiving") or active valuing?
- Does it wish to encourage particular values or attitudes, or to bring about a major change in viewpoint?
- Do the objectives reflect the levels of performance found in instructional activities called for by the program?

TABLE 1
An Annotated Cognitive Domain Taxonomy*

This classification describes, from simplest to most complex, six degrees to which information that is taught can be learned.

1. **Knowledge.** *Recalling information pretty much as it was learned.*
   In its simplest manifestation, this includes knowledge of the terminology and specific facts–dates, people, etc.–associated with an area of subject matter. At a more complex level it means knowing the major sub-areas, methods of inquiry, classifications and ways of thinking characteristic of the subject area, as well as its central theories and principles.

2. **Comprehension.** *Reporting information in a way other than how it was learned in order to show that it has been understood.*
   Most basically this means reporting something learned through an alternative medium. More complex evidence of comprehension involves interpreting information in "one's own words" or in some other original way, or extrapolating from it to new but related ideas and implications.

3. **Application.** *Use of learned information to solve a problem.*
   This means carrying over knowledge of facts or methods learned in one specific context to completely new ones.

4. **Analysis.** *Taking learned information apart.*
   Analysis means figuring out a subject matter's most elemental ideas and their interrelationships.

5. **Synthesis.** *Creating something new–and good, based on some criterion.*
   This creation can be something that communicates to an audience, that plans a successful goal-directed endeavor, or that subsumes a collection of ideas within a new theory.

6. **Evaluation.** *Judging the value of something for a particular purpose.*
   This means making a statement of something's worth based either on one's own well-developed criteria or on the well-understood criteria of another.

*Adapted from *TAXONOMY OF EDUCATIONAL OBJECTIVES: The Classification of Educational Goals: HANDBOOK 1: Cognitive Domain,* by Benjamin S. Bloom, et al. Copyright ©1956 by Longman Inc. Previously published by David McKay Company, Inc. By permission of Longman Inc.

In those cases where you as evaluator are asked to offer an opinion of the quality of the program's aims themselves, you might use the taxonomies as a guide in formulating your response. Ask yourself:

- Does the program contain a sufficient number of high-level objectives, given its time frame and the group of students for whom it is intended?

TABLE 2

An Annotated Affective Domain Taxonomy*

This classification describes the various ways in which a person might display an attitude about something. A good way to think of this list is as a progression in the person's willingness to have some phenomenon (an event, a body of subject matter, a person, etc.) affect him. The list describes levels of behavior from barest exposure to deep involvement.

1. **Receiving.** *Paying attention.*
   Most basically, this means just knowing that something exists or is going on. It also includes alert watching and listening.
2. **Responding.** *Active exploration or participation.*
   At base, responding means not-necessarily-enthusiastic willingness to take part in something. A more developed manifestation includes satisfaction, pleasure, or even pursuit of a certain activity, person or thing.
3. **Valuing.** *Consistent behavior showing positive regard for something.*
   This might mean behavior in keeping with advice from others about the right—but not necessary pleasurable—route to a desired goal. At a deeper level, it involves commitment, expression of a particular point-of-view, and assuming responsibilities.
4. **Organization.** *Building and behaving according to a single set of life principles.*
   Organization includes holding consistent points-of-view about many aspects of life, without contradictions or conflict.
5. **Characterization by a value or value complex.** *Being predictable.*
   This means showing a strongly detectable—and effective—pattern of growth or adjustment to life in general.

*Adapted from *TAXONOMY OF EDUCATIONAL OBJECTIVES: The Classification of Educational Goals: Handbook 2: Affective Domain,* by David R. Krathwohl, et al. Copyright ©1964 by Longman Inc. Previously published by David McKay Company, Inc. By permission of Longman Inc.

Principle No. 3: Objectives may be written for a whole program as well as for individuals

You have probably noticed that sometimes objectives refer to goals for a whole program. For instance:

> Eighty percent of the students shall score above the 50th percentile on the Iowa Test of Educational Development.

This objective does refer to observable student behavior—test-taking—which is specified in detail in the manual for the administration of the test chosen for the program.

So far, the objectives discussed in this booklet have referred to single students since single-student objectives *are* most used (and useful) for writing tests. Larger-scale behavioral objectives are often used as well, however, to express the aims of the overall program, and, like the single-student objectives, they describe observable outcomes. The difference is that they specify what observable evidence will be accepted as proof that the *program* has succeeded.

By definition, behavioral objectives as goal statements for the whole program will outline the criteria that must be met in order for the program to be judged effective. In the example above, program *success* demands a 50th percentile score, or higher, from 80% of the students. Of course, such clear-cut criteria for success will, in most cases, be impossible to justify. This will be particularly the case with attitude or affective goals. You should use a behavioral statement of a program goal only when you find that in your situation such a criterion for the program is reasonable. It is worth noting, however, that the behavioral statement of a goal for the whole program has an obvious advantage; it simplifies your job as evaluator by pinpointing exactly what evidence will determine program success.

Principle No. 4: In wording the objective, the verb should be concrete

Since a behavioral objective needs to specify a response on the part of the student, and since the response has to be *observable* (again, it will be your proof that the student has the desired skill), the verb must denote an *action*. Therefore, the following verbs are to be avoided:

know	appreciate	enjoy
understand	comprehend	

as well as:

demonstrate	identify	distinguish

Though these last three are actions of a sort, they are still too ambiguous to be useful for describing what a test should look like. Much more preferable are:

write	list	build
choose from a list	sort	compare
say aloud	point to	volunteer

At times, the stimulus to be presented will be so well specified that the rule about action verbs in the response section of the objectives can be relaxed. Such is the case with objectives like

> Given the Comprehensive Test of Basic Skills, the student will achieve scores typical of his/her grade level, or better.
>
> Given an electronic calculator, the student will use it to compute a square root.

Ask yourself whether you can picture the action to be performed by the student in your mind's eye. If you can, the objective is adequately concrete and should be measurable.

Attitude and affective objectives present unique objectives-writing problems. *Attitudes are hard to describe in behavioral terms.* If measurement instruments are to be developed to evaluate attainment of attitude goals, however, it is critical that objectives be clearly specified. Someone must decide how a person who has attained a desirable level of the attitude in question would behave. If this cannot be done, or if agreement among planners cannot be achieved, then you should question whether the goal is worth including as a primary focus of the evaluation. Attempting to measure an ambiguous attitude will ultimately open the evaluation to criticism. The best way to "behaviorize" an attitude objective is to have people who should know (program planners, child development experts) provide scenarios of situations in which people high and low in the attitude in question would behave differently. Write objectives that describe, if possible, behaviors such as these. In the interest of planning measurement instruments, decide on the level of behavioral evidence you will be willing to accept:

- If the evaluation audience will likely be satisfied with a self-report, you might simply include the words "say" or "report" in the behavioral objective. For example: "Given pre- and post-program attitude toward school questionnaires, the student will report an increasingly positive attitude."
- If people will only believe reports of actual behavior, then measures will have to be observational, and behavioral objectives should be written accordingly.

Writing attitude objectives is often made simpler by working from examples. Ask to see the objectives written to underpin projects similar to yours. Or select from the commercially available objectives collections mentioned in Chapter 2.

Principle No. 5: The stimulus and response portions of the objective should be as explicit and detailed as possible, even to the extent of containing sample test items

Behavioral objectives that will help you evaluate student performance should clearly describe

(a) the stimulus demands that will be made upon students,
(b) the exact form the response or performance should take, and
(c) the criteria by which the adequacy of the performance will be determined.

In other words, since the objective describes a test, the closer it can come to exact specifications, the better.

Consider the writing objective:

> Given directions, the student will write a paragraph developed by means of comparison and contrast.

This objective is clear enough for many purposes. As a guide for the teachers, it means that a unit must be included in the curriculum aimed at communicating an idea by contrasting attributes of various people, events or objects. As a basis for a test, however, the objective leaves many questions unanswered: What sort of directions will the student receive? What constraints will be placed on the task, e.g., will reference books be available or not? How long should the paragraph be? What should be contrasted–ideas such as liberalism and conservatism, or concrete objects like collies and German shepherds? How will the adequacy of the paragraph be judged?

We can improve the writing objective by reformulating it as if it were a recipe for a test. One example might be:

> Given a dictionary and two wordless comic strips describing two different personal problems and how they were dealt with, the student will write a paragraph pointing out three similarities and three differences between two such personal-problem situations (or how they were handled), and will make one introductory or summary observation in the paragraph. Paragraphs will be judged separately on communication (the

presence of the seven mentioned content features) and on grammar.

The student will be informed in the instructions for the task that attempting to use compound sentences in making the comparisons and contrasts will possibly enhance his or her grammar score, and cannot detract from either score. The student will also be informed that a problem situation of his or her own knowledge or invention may be substituted for just one of the two pictorial situations.

The paragraph meets the criterion for passing in terms of communication if it includes at least five of the seven content features called for. Each paragraph will be graded independently by three teachers, and the results will be averaged. This will allow for different judgments as to whether a statement in the paragraph lacked common sense or was merely repetitious of the meaning of a previous statement, and should therefore not be counted. In any student's paragraph, the maximum number of similarities to be counted is three, and the maximum number of introductory or summary statements is one.

Passing in terms of grammar will depend on which of two computed numbers is greater. The first number is the sum of the number of correctly formed compound sentences plus the number of predicates (the latter reflects paragraph length). The second number is twice the number of grammatical errors in the paragraph. (Only those kinds of errors cited on a predetermined list will be counted, and errors related to forming a compound sentence will be ignored.) In order to pass in terms of grammar, the first number must be greater than the second.

This example is presented only as a possibility. Regardless of the merit of the task or criteria described, there is no question but that this objective gives a clearer picture of the skills called for than does the previous objective, and such an increase in clarity and specificity will bring you that much closer to a basis for constructing or selecting an appropriate test.

Even so, this objective could have been made still more specific. For example, more could have been said about the stimuli—the directions, the picture characteristics, and the possible use of sample items to illustrate what constitutes a satisfactory answer. Another constraint, the *time limit*, was not mentioned. Finally, in the criteria, the list of the types of grammatical *errors* that will be graded could be either referenced (if from a published source) or enumerated.

Much discussion in the recent evaluation literature has centered on possible methods for making behavioral objectives *unambiguous* and *more specific*[7] in order to ensure that they will specify test items that show mastery of the objective. Out of this discussion has come the proposal to state objectives even more precisely than the currently used format, *Given . . . the student will. . . .* If you intend eventually to write test items, any of the following methods of writing specific behavioral objectives may be used:

1. Where the subject matter allows (e.g., mathematics, phonics), you can use items themselves as objectives. For example:

```
              MATH OBJECTIVE X

    Subtraction such as:
                   5 - 3 =
                   7 - 2 =

    8 items.  Passing = 7 correct.
```

   Writing the objective in this way defines a class of problems and displays a format for their presentation. Test writers should be able to infer further items from it. Using this format, the objective is a recipe for the test. Here is another example:

```
            READING OBJECTIVE Y

  Read CVC trigrams ending in "AN":
                 CAN
                 DAN, etc.

  10 items.  Passing = 9 correct.
```

7. If you are interested in consulting the considerable literature on this topic, procedures for stating objectives that serve as a basis for test items are generally discussed under the heading of "domain specification." Some references to help you learn more appear in the section "For Further Reading" at the end of the chapter.

2. Behavioral objectives for most subject areas can be clearly formatted in terms of (a) instructions, (b) test stimuli and/or materials, and (c) the necessary *correct* student responses. An example:

```
                    HISTORY OBJECTIVE Z

Instructions:   Decide whether the following statements are
                true or false.

Stimuli:        Ten true-or-false statements of causes of
                the Revolutionary War.

Response:       Student writes true beside true statements,
                false beside false ones.

                Passing criterion--9 correct.
```

3. A third alternative method for writing behavioral objectives is to retain the *Given . . . the student will . . .* format, but to increase the specificity of the stimuli and responses it names. Such an objective would look like this:

```
                    MATH OBJECTIVE N

Given two fractions with different denominators, where one
denominator is divisible by the other (e.g., 5/6 and 2/3),
the student will correctly convert the fraction with the
smaller denominator, and add.

Criterion for passing--12 correct out of 15 items.

Half credit for answers left as improper fraction or not
in lowest terms.
```

How should you decide which of the various methods of writing objectives is most appropriate for your program? This depends partly, of course, on the objectives format habitually used by or desirable to your teachers and test writers. Another consideration in choosing a method is the requirements for writing objectives that have been given to you. Only

Method No. 3 yields objectives that look like what people will expect to see when they request behavioral objectives, while Methods No. 1 and No. 2 provide objectives that more closely resemble the test.

To illustrate this, Math Objective N might be reformatted as follows:

MATH OBJECTIVE N
(Method No. 1 Format)

Addition of two proper fractions using lowest common denominator:

5/9 + 2/3 =
3/4 + 1/12 =

15 items. Criterion for passing: 12 correct.

Note: One denominator is a multiple of the other. Half credit for an otherwise correct answer left as an improper fraction (e.g., 10/6) or not in lowest terms (e.g., 1 4/6).

MATH OBJECTIVE N
(Method No. 2 Format)

Instructions: Add the following fractions. Be sure to find the lowest common denominator.

Stimuli: 15 problems written in equation form, each a sum of two proper fractions, such that one denominator is divisible by the other (e.g., 5/6 + 2/3 =).

Response: Student first finds lowest common denominator, converts one fraction, adds. Correct answers should be expressed in lowest terms and not left as improper fractions; otherwise, half credit is given (e.g., if an answer should be 1 1/2, half credit would be given for either 9/6 or 1 3/6).

Passing criterion--12 correct.

A few words about correctness criteria: the format for writing objectives described here assumes that scorers of the test will have available a simple way to distinguish correct answers. For tests requiring a "closed" response–multiple-choice, true-false, matching, etc.–correctness is easy to determine. Objectives describing complex skills or attitudes often demand "open-ended" responses such as essays, short answers, or observed performance. Scoring these is difficult. When possible, however, criteria describing correct and incorrect responses should be included in the statement of the objective. In situations when you demand an essay, or enactment of a procedure (such as balancing on a narrow board or dismantling a carburetor), follow these suggestions, then make sure the eventual test scorers know about your decisions:

1. Define good performance in terms of speed or quality, or both. A third-grade penmanship objective, for instance, might look like this:

```
HANDWRITING OBJECTIVE R

Student writes five 20-word sentences from dictation.  Is
instructed to write as fast as legibility will allow.  Per-
mitted three minutes per sentence.

Criterion:  Of the 100 words, no more than 10 will be
omitted or illegible (as determined by scorer's judgment).
```

2. In some situations where you wish to justify the criteria used, you may be able to obtain from the research literature, from the experience of a handy expert, or from a published list of professional standards a description of speed, accuracy or quality of performance that fits the age and ability of the group in question. When you obtain such a description, it can be used to make a list of criteria, and you should train scorers to use them. For instance, a list of criteria for judging the quality of a paragraph developed by comparison and contrast might read as follows:

```
Criteria.  To be judged correct, the paragraph must:

1.  Compare at least four attributes of the two subjects
    in question

2.  Cite points of both resemblance and difference

3.  Have one of three formats:

    a.  Subject A (e.g., liberalism) is described fully,
        followed by a complete description of Subject B
        (e.g., conservatism) with contrasting attributes
        described in the same order

    b.  Attributes are listed, and A and B compared
        immediately

    c.  A mixture of both
```

Where criteria are too complex to enumerate, *obtain credible judges* to assess general adequacy of response.

Reconciling Objectives and Standardized Tests

In spite of the vitality of the trend to aim program evaluation and curriculum planning toward announced objectives, the instruments used in many state and district assessment programs continue to be standardized[8] tests. Since these tests are administered as a matter of course, using them as a basis for evaluation could save time and trouble. In many cases, also, using standardized tests allows the evaluator to talk about achievement in a context with which school personnel and the general public are familiar. There are two ways, of course, to ensure that standardized tests and program objectives coincide: fit the objectives to the test, or analyze the test according to the objectives.

---

8. In this booklet, "standardized" refers to tests that are not criterion-referenced. This follows the common usage of the term, though it is recognized that criterion-referenced tests can be "standardized" in terms of strict adherence to explicit procedures of administration and scoring.

How to Derive Objectives from Standardized Tests

School districts often want to show an improvement in the scores on the standardized tests that are given each year as part of the state or local assessment program. Recently in California and New York, for example, such test scores were published in newspapers making the results of standardized tests increasingly important to principals and parents. What sort of direct action could be taken to improve scores on these tests? Clearly, teaching students the test items would invalidate the test, undermining its purpose. Both ethically and legally, the district cannot show the tests to the teachers in time for them to teach the students the items on the test. Publishers who have spent thousands of dollars to develop standardized tests sell them to school districts with the understanding that the security of the tests will in no way be violated.

Is there another way to design instruction so as to produce higher student scores on standardized achievement tests? One solution to this problem that is both legal and fair is to teach toward the objectives that underlie the test. There is a simple procedure for "psyching out" these objectives:

1. Have one person, for example, yourself or a district office curriculum consultant, obtain a copy of the appropriate level of the achievement test with which the school or a particular program is going to be concerned.
2. Have the items from the test typed on cards, or cut up the test and paste one item on each card.
3. Assemble these cards on a desk in front of you, and put the items into groups which appear to cover similar material.
4. When the standardized achievement test has been reduced to about 30 groups of items, write objectives that characterize the stimulus, response, and correctness criteria for each of these groups. Then generate items *similar* to those on the test as sample items for the objectives. *The objectives must not include any items that are actually copies of the ones on the test.*
5. Give the list of objectives and sample items for those objectives to teachers and curriculum developers for use in program planning. The objectives will provide a focus for instructional activity during the school year without violating the security of the test. Teachers can then direct special effort to teaching the objectives that the achievement test measures, without ever seeing the items on the test.

The teachers and the curriculum director may, of course, find that they need many objectives in addition to those derived from the achievement test. Perhaps, for instance, an objective on the achievement test cannot be met until certain preceding objectives have been achieved by the students. In this situation, curriculum planning will have to extend to skill levels prerequisite to those defined by the goals of the achievement test. Analysis of the test can, however, provide a goal for the program: students must develop, among others, skills reflected by the objectives of the standardized achievement test.

The question of whether it is desirable to generate educational goals from standardized achievement tests is controversial. Some humanists, for instance, deplore this as "teaching to the test," and it is indeed conceivable that such a practice, if improperly understood, might narrow the curriculum to the point of overemphasis on piecemeal skills. It is not suggested, however, that the objectives identified from the test form the *sole* basis for the curriculum. They should simply be included in curriculum planning. It is, after all, unfair to expect students to perform well on a test whose objectives have not been communicated. When a decision is made to use a standardized achievement test, the implication is that the objectives measured by that test either already are part of the curriculum, or should be. Otherwise, why give a test that has nothing to do with what is supposed to be taught? The approach described in this chapter, then, constitutes one kind of shift away from haphazard curricular policies toward a greater emphasis on goals whose importance is widely acknowledged.

Using a Standardized Test to Evaluate a Program

Since standardized achievement tests are often given routinely, they present a constantly available source of data for the evaluation of programs. A standardized test is useful for program evaluation, however, only to the extent that it:

1. Contains items which measure the objectives addressed by the program
2. Includes enough of these items to provide a valid measure of each objective's accomplishment (at least five items per objective)

The more general your objectives, the more likely it is that any specific test will satisfy these two criteria. If you are working with individual student behavioral objectives, however, you will probably find that the standardized test, failing to meet criterion No. 2 for nearly all objectives, will be an unacceptable measure of program results. You will probably receive a fairer picture of what the program accomplished if you purchase or construct a criterion-referenced test that is based on the objectives of your program.

If you know that a certain standardized test will be administered to the program's students, and you believe that the test does, in part, measure some of your program goals, you might decide to use the test results as one indicator of program effectiveness. In this case, your task will be to extract information about how students performed on *just those test items relevant to the program you are evaluating.* The procedure for extracting such information, though it may be time-consuming, is straightforward:

1. Obtain a copy of the test that will be administered, and, if you can, cut up the test and paste each item on a separate card. Otherwise, have the items typed on cards.
2. Have someone who is very familiar with the program sort the items into piles labeled

	MODERATELY	NOT
APPROPRIATE	APPROPRIATE	APPROPRIATE

   Items that measure program objectives belong in the first pile, while those that do not reflect program goals at all belong in the pile labeled "not appropriate." Items that for any reason, including formatting or disparate wording, are not entirely suitable for evaluating the program should be placed in the "moderately appropriate" pile. If the task proves difficult or you feel that the reliability of one person's judgment is not adequate, have several judges sort the items and resolve differences through discussion. If the number of test items in the "appropriate" category is judged too small to provide any reliable indication of your program's success, then do not use the test in your program evaluation.
3. Designate the items in the three groups "subtests." Make a list of item numbers for each subtest, and plan to analyze the three subtests separately when the test is scored.
4. Use as an indicator of program success the mean score of all students in the program on the subtest composed of the most appropriate items. Depending on the thoroughness of the score-reporting service you receive, this mean can be calculated in one of two ways:

   a. If time is short, or if the agency scoring the standardized test does not provide an item-by-item breakdown of students' scores, the relevant test items should be scored by hand *before* the tests are sent off for data processing. Add up item results for each student in the program on the relevant subtest and from these subtest scores compute the average score for program students.

b. If the agency scoring the test does provide a calculation, "percent correct" for program students on each test item, then you may save yourself some trouble by waiting for the printout. When it arrives, list this percent for each item in the subtest as a decimal (e.g., 83% becomes .83). Just add these decimals to obtain the average raw score of the students on the subtest.[9]

5. Similarly, obtain the mean score of program students on the other two subtests if you want some idea of what transfer of learning may have resulted from the program. That is, the program may have indirectly improved students' performance on items calling for skills somewhat related to the program, or even outside the primary focus of the program.

If you have available item results from the same test for students who are *not* receiving any instruction aimed at your program's goals, you

---

9. Why does summing the decimals give you the average *raw* score? Because calculating the raw score from percents correct per item demands first dividing the sum of the percents by the number of items to get the average percent correct, and then multiplying again by this number to convert the average percent correct to a raw score. The operations of dividing and then multiplying by the same number cancel each other.

Consider this example. A test has *five* items. Percent of the students getting each item correct is as follows:

Item	*Percent of students getting item correct*	*Translated to decimals*
1	80%	.80
2	25%	.25
3	35%	.35
4	90%	.90
5	40%	.40

5/2.70 = sum of decimals

.54 = mean percent correct over five items

To determine the average raw score from the five items, you must multiply .54 by 5. You get 2.70 again.

should save such data for possible use in making comparisons of results on the three subtests.

If you have an evaluation design that seeks to compare the effectiveness of two programs in teaching goals that are common to both and if these goals are also addressed by items on the standardized achievement test used by your district, two changes in the procedure are called for:

1. The three piles for sorting items need to be re-labeled as, say:

APPROPRIATE FOR BOTH PROGRAMS	MODERATELY APPROPRIATE FOR BOTH PROGRAMS	REJECTED

   There must, of course, be enough items in the first pile if the test results are to be useful to your comparison. "Rejected" here means that an item was found to be completely unaddressed by one or the other program. Results from such items will not be used in your comparison of the effectiveness of the two programs in teaching the same goals.

2. Item results for students in different programs must be kept separate, so that mean subtest scores can be computed separately for students in different programs.

Great caution is necessary in drawing conclusions from standardized test results if you should decide to use them. You should keep in mind that item selection methods for standardized tests lead publishers to include slightly tricky items that might not give an accurate picture of skill mastery. Another problem comes from the extent of overlap of test and program. *Any specific standardized test can only be expected to cover a subset, perhaps a small subset, of the objectives of a particular program.* Therefore, success with the objectives covered by the standardized test cannot be relied on for a comprehensive measure of the worth of the program as a whole. Any test can only measure the success of the students in achieving the objectives covered by it, and both the limited range of objectives and the limited number of items per objective usually make a standardized test a weak instrument for assessing program effects.

The procedure outlined here represents a fair way of using a standardized test to measure the achievement of some program objectives. In many cases, the amount of information it provides will be too incomplete to justify the time and effort involved. However, it is one source of information about the program and can be useful if used with appropriate caution.

For Further Reading

On the topic of writing objectives . . .

Davies, I. K. *Competency-based learning: Technology, management, and design.* Chapter 5: Writing objectives. New York: McGraw-Hill, 1973.

Gronlund, N. E. *Stating behavioral objectives for classroom instruction.* New York: Macmillan Publishing Co., 1970.

Lee, B. N., & Merrill, M. D. *Writing complete affective objectives: A short course.* Belmont, CA: Wadsworth, 1972.

Mager, R. F. *Preparing instructional objectives* (2nd ed.). Belmont, CA: Fearon Publishers, 1962.

Pierce, W. D., & Lorber, M. A. *Objectives and methods for secondary teaching,* Englewood Cliffs, NJ: Prentice Hall, 1977.

Concerning standardized tests for evaluations . . .

Cox, R. C., & Sterrett, B. G. A model for increasing the meaning of standardized test scores. *Journal of Educational Measurement,* 1970, 7, 227-228.

On the topic of domain specification . . .

Gronlund, N. E. *Preparing criterion-referenced tests for classroom instruction.* New York: Macmillan Publishing Co., 1973.

Hively, W., et al. *Domain-referenced curriculum evaluation: A technical handbook and a case study from the Minnemast project.* Los Angeles: Center for the Study of Evaluation, University of California, 1973.

Popham, W. J. *Criterion-referenced measurement.* Englewood Cliffs, NJ: Prentice-Hall, 1977.

Chapter 4

Assigning Priorities to Objectives

People who plan programs usually want their programs to accomplish many objectives. Very often, however, the evaluator has neither the time nor the resources to measure the accomplishment of all these desired objectives. A decision must therefore be made: Which objectives should serve as the focus for the evaluation? In addition, a person developing a test or attitude questionnaire might generate too many items to administer conveniently at a single sitting. What is the best way to ensure that the test will truly represent the subject matter being assessed, that the most important questions will be asked, and that the students and testing staff will not be overburdened?

Answers to these problems can be found in careful random sampling or systematic identification of a representative set of objectives or items.

Several techniques are available to assist the evaluator with sampling and prioritizing objectives. A summary of these solutions is found in Table 3. Solutions 1, 2, and 3 prescribe sampling from the total pool of objectives. Solution 1 involves simple random sampling; Solution 2 samples from among those judged by independent raters to be the most important; and Solution 3 describes *matrix sampling,* a technique which is becoming increasingly popular where multitudes of objectives must be assessed. Solutions 4 and 5 describe methods for ranking objectives in order of importance by either asking people's opinions (Solution 4) or constructing hierarchies (Solution 5).

TABLE 3. Solutions to the

Method	Quick Summary	Advantages
1. Sampling objectives	Randomly select objectives from the total set.	• Can be done by the evaluator alone–without cooperation from others. • The quickest, simplest method. • Treats all program objectives–on the test or not–as instructionally important.
2. Sampling the important objectives	Two or three raters select the few objectives they think are most important. From this pool, objectives are then randomly chosen, if necessary.	• Fairly fast method. • Gives people (the raters) a say in the evaluation. • Makes it unlikely that important objectives will be missed.
3. Matrix Sampling	*All* objectives are used. They are assigned to parts of a test, and each part is given to a randomly selected group of students.	• Can be done by the evaluator alone–without cooperation from others. • All objectives are tested, albeit with samples of students rather than all students.
4. Assigning priorities to all objectives through ratings (Retrospective needs assessment)	A group of approximately 15 raters rate all objectives according to a 5-point scale. Mean ratings determine priorities.	• Yields accurate assessment of the priorities of interest groups represented by the raters. • Involves raters in the evaluation and is therefore likely to increase credibility.
5. Assigning priorities through objectives hierarchies	Objectives grouped into content areas, then charted from simple to complex. The more complex or "terminal" ones receive highest priority.	• Can be done by the evaluator alone–without cooperation from others. • Assigns priority to the most logically complex objectives, avoiding attention to too simple ones.

Problem of Too Many Objectives

Disadvantages	Recommendations
• The risk exists of missing objectives or items that might be important thus reducing the credibility of the evaluation.	Highly recommended when all objectives are of about equal importance.
• Focuses evaluation on a small number of objectives. • Depends on cooperation of raters. • Raters' choices may not represent opinions of other concerned persons.	Highly recommended when you have credible raters available and objectives which are not all of equal importance, and feel you will be able to narrow down to as few as 10 objectives measured by 50 items.
• Somewhat involved procedure • Data not entirely appropriate for use with some statistical tests.	The only method by which you can assess all objectives. Due to the procedure's complexity, however, use it only when you cannot avoid testing all objectives or items.
• Focuses evaluation on a small number of objectives. • Depends on cooperation of raters. • Time-consuming for evaluators and raters.	A good procedure to use, if you have time for it and can gain cooperation from enough raters. Especially recommended when the acceptance of the evaluation by various groups is a major concern.
• Relatively time-consuming, depending on the number of objectives. • It may not be desirable to test only terminal, difficult objectives.	Probably should be used only when you, as evaluator, must narrow down the number of objectives yourself, without assistance, and when the subject matter lends itself to logical hierarchies.

It may be noted that, while these solutions are phrased in terms of objectives, the word "items" may be substituted for "objectives" in Solutions 1 through 4, since they can be applied as well to the construction of a test from a pool of items that have not been classified according to the objectives they measure. However, since the evaluation of the program must eventually be made in terms of the evidence that certain objectives were achieved, you will surely want to avoid constructing a test without first attending to what objectives it measures.

Also keep in mind that Solutions 4 and 5 are useful for focussing an evaluation even when the ultimate aim is not to narrow down a large number of objectives or items for testing. It is equally important, since time and funds are limited, to expend the greatest effort on examining what is most important in terms of the constituents' values and in terms of the structure of the subject taught. In the same vein, at some early point in the evaluation, you should certainly *consult program staff about which of their announced objectives they realistically expect to accomplish.* If the program has received funding based on a proposal, chances are that the objectives in the proposal promise more than the program can hope to accomplish.

Solution 1: Sampling Objectives

The quickest way to narrow down the number of objectives or items to be included in a test is to choose some at random from the larger pool and base the test on the fairly representative sample thus selected.

Simple random sampling of objectives is a legitimate way of scaling down the size of a test for program evaluation. Furthermore, by letting it be known that the final outcome will consist of a random sample of objectives, all objectives retain importance to teachers since the items from any objective could appear on the test. This ensures less chance of teachers or other program managers deciding to teach only to a few of the objectives.

Simple random sampling, however, might lead to problems with the credibility of the evaluation. There is the possibility that by randomly discarding objectives, you will be throwing out some that the program planners or the funding agency personnel or other involved people feel are particularly important to the evaluation. This eventuality could lead them to say, "Your results are useless, because you didn't test for the most important skills we wanted to teach." Solution 2 uses a simple rating scheme that serves to answer such an objection.

Solution 2: Sampling the Important Objectives

Solution 2 relies on ranking objectives according to their importance and then sampling from the most important ones to form a test. Though this sampling method does rely on ratings, it is more convenient to use than Solution 4, which assigns priorities to *all* of the objectives on the basis of combined opinions of different constituent groups.

Instructions for reducing test size by rating and randomizing. This procedure directs the selection of 10 objectives. You will want to select more or fewer depending on the size of the test you construct. Remember that each objective means five test items. (Note, too, that if you use this procedure to rate and select items rather than objectives, you will want to extend the process in order to form a test with more than 10 items.)

1. Contact raters for the objectives. These can be the two or three persons most familiar with the program you are evaluating, or those who know the most about what the program was to accomplish, or the people who have to be convinced by your results. Only if you cannot find raters, and you yourself are sufficiently familiar with the program should the rating be done by you alone.

2. Give each rater a set of the program objectives written on cards, one objective to a card. You may give them a list of objectives, but this makes rating more difficult. Make sure that the objectives are all roughly equal in level of generality. Raters, it has been shown, will rate general objectives higher than specific ones, regardless of their feelings about the relative importance of the subject matter. Instruct raters to *rank order* the objectives according to *how important it is that the objective be tested by the test.* The end product of their work should be a pile of objectives with the one they feel most crucial for the test on top, the next most important under it, etc. Let raters determine *their own criteria* for rating. Otherwise, you could become involved in lengthy arguments over whether to consult learning hierarchies, or whether to choose by more subjective means. Since your raters are people intimately involved with the program, they will have many complex and interrelated reasons to back up their opinions about which of its objectives should be tested.

3. Once you have collected the rated objectives from each rater (set a firm deadline), select the top 10 from each. (If you have only one rater, this person's choice of 10 will comprise the test.) Deal out all 10 cards from each rater and look for matches among raters. Raters' objectives that match should definitely become part of the test.

4. Assemble the 10 objectives that will comprise the test:

(a) Set aside the objectives that have been selected by the raters. How many are there? Subtract this amount from 10. The remainder is the number of objectives you have yet to select.

(b) Find the objectives that have been selected by all but one rater. How many are there? Does this number bring your objectives to 10? If it does, you have your complete test! However, if you still have less than 10 objectives, go to substep c which follows. If you now have more than 10 objectives, go to substep d.

(c) If you still have fewer than 10 objectives, count how many more objectives you need, and select this number at random from the remaining objectives given you by the raters.

(d) If you now have more than 10 objectives, randomly eliminate as many as necessary so that you go back to 10. To do this, shuffle all the objectives cards that were selected by all but one rater; then randomly select out the ones you need to eliminate.

5. You are now ready to write the test based on the 10 objectives you have selected. The test that results from objective sampling is a good response to the problem of too many objectives. And the rating of objectives has allowed you to consider the priorities of people important to your evaluation in constructing the evaluation instrument.

Solution 3: Matrix Sampling

Should you find it absolutely necessary to test every objective or to use every item, then matrix sampling offers a method for doing so by randomly sampling students. Matrix sampling involves a combination of procedures for randomly selecting students and for assigning items to test forms.

In matrix sampling, students are randomly assigned to take parts of a single large test. These parts are, in turn, composed of objectives and items that have been randomly assigned from the original large pool. It functions as follows: one sample of students takes one sample of objectives, a second takes a second sample of objectives, and so forth. An example of matrix sampling is shown in Figure 1.

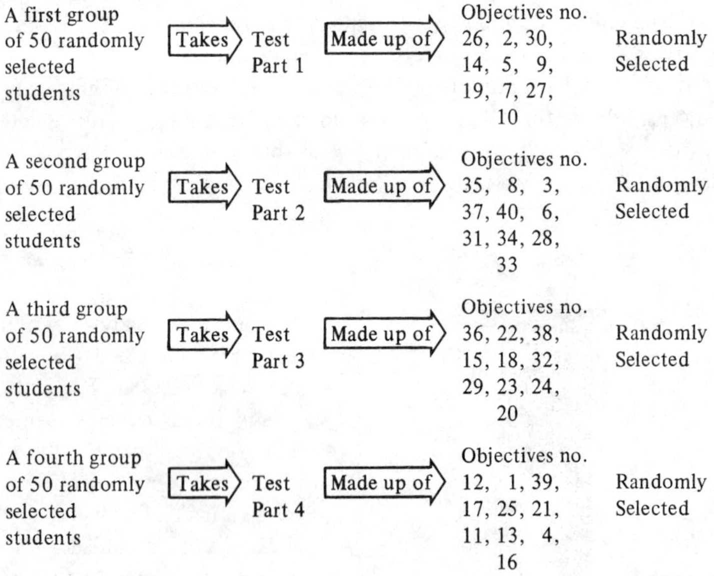

Figure 1. An example of matrix sampling assignments of 200 students and 40 objectives. Each student will take a 50 item test.

Figure 1 shows that 200 students have been randomly divided into four groups to take four parts of a 40-objective test (10 objectives per part). Students have been assigned to groups, and objectives have been numbered and assigned to test parts. Thus, a student who has randomly fallen into the third group for testing will receive part three, composed of objectives 36, 22, 38, 15, 18, 32, 29, 23, 24, and 20, all randomly assigned. This student will receive a 50-item test covering these 10 objectives, five items per objective.

What if 10 objectives is too long a test for the given subject matter, or for these particular students? In this case, the evaluator could have constructed eight student groups of 25 students each to take test parts containing only five objectives (or 25 items). Or, ultimately, 40 tests, each based on just one of the objectives, could have been given to 40 groups of 5 students each. This last alternative, though feasible, is not the best way to do matrix sampling. A good rule of thumb to follow is to set up sampling so that students take the longest test they can manage. *The more objectives each single student receives, the better.* It moves the matrix-sampling situation closer to the ideal of obtaining data that are based on every student's performance on every objective.

You have no doubt noticed that where matrix sampling is used, no one student is tested on all the objectives of a program. Ten objectives is about the most any particular student is tested on. This is why single-student data obtained through matrix sampling are of limited use. *Matrix-sampling data tell you little about the achievement of individual students.* Matrix sampling is only useful for measuring the achievement of a group. Group information, however, is exactly what is necessary for program evaluation. On a test divided into five parts, each part would be taken by a different group of students in a matrix sample. If each part covered six objectives, then test results from the five randomly chosen groups would reflect the whole test of 30 objectives. Since they were randomly selected, the student groups taking test parts can be said to produce test results that are representative of the results you would get if all the students took the whole test. That is, given many students, all randomly assigned to take test parts, you will be able to state quite reliably that the results you obtain through matrix sampling are the same as those you would have if every student had been tested on all the items.

A note to those of you who are interested in statistics: matrix sampling is entirely appropriate for estimating the true *mean* score of a group of students. If you wish to perform statistical tests using data from matrix sampling, however, you should bear in mind that matrix-sample estimates of variance of scores are sometimes far from the true variance. For this reason, we encourage you *not* to use matrix sampling if you are planning to use your test data to perform statistical tests. Nevertheless, you can effectively use data from matrix sampling for *graphing* results, say, the percent of students passing each item or objective, with the admonition that you should not consider small differences significant.

A limitation of matrix sampling. Of course, even using matrix sampling will not allow you to have an infinity of objectives or items. The number of objectives or items you can use for matrix sampling will depend on the number of students available for testing. Below is a process that will help you estimate the number of objectives you will be able to test in your situation:

> Ask yourself: Can the students for whom the test is intended manage a test covering 10 objectives?
>
> If so, then in order to matrix-sample, you must have available for testing at least as many students (students per program if you have experimental and control groups) as you have objectives. If you have more objectives than students, you cannot matrix-sample.
>
> If not, that is, if individual students cannot take a 10-objective test because the test will run too long, then you must have proportionately more students.
>
> If students can only take a 5-objective test, which is half the usual size, then you will need at least twice as many students as objectives.
>
> If students can only take a 3-objective test, which is roughly one-third the usual size, then you will need at least three times as many students as objectives.

It is also possible, by a different process, to determine whether you have enough students to matrix-sample based on the number of items each student can handle.

> Ask yourself: Can the students for whom the test is intended manage a 50-item test?

If so, then divide the number of items you have by 5 to determine the minimum number of students you will need in order to matrix-sample.[10]

If not, that is, if individual students could not manage a 50-item test because of age or subject matter, then recalculate the minimum number of students you will need.

If they can handle 40-items, then the minimum number of students necessary is equal to the total number of items, divided by 4.

If they can manage only 30-items, the minimum number of students is total items, divided by 3.

If they can manage 10, the minimum number of students should equal the total number of items. If students can manage only five items, you will need twice the number of students as you have items.

Please notice that the procedures described above do not determine absolute numbers of students necessary for matrix sampling. They give you minimums. Actually, *the more students you have per objective or item, the better;* this will make the matrix-sampling situation closer to the ideal testing situation (where all students provide you with data about their performance on every objective), the results of which you are *estimating.*

Instructions for matrix sampling. Below is a step-by-step procedure for matrix sampling.

1. Determine how many groups, and therefore matrix samples, you will need. Make sure that you are clear about exactly how many groups you will be discussing in the evaluation. Will you be comparing an experimental and a control group? Will you compare results per grade level?

10. This prescription is based on the following reasoning: you must have at least *ten* students for every *part* of the test you administer. The number of parts, of course, will equal the number of items, divided by the number of items per part. So, if there are 50 items on each part, the necessary number of students will equal:

$$\frac{\text{total number of items X 10}}{50} \quad \text{or} \quad \frac{\text{total number of items}}{5}$$

For each group from which you wish to collect test results, you will need to do a separate matrix sampling. And for each matrix sampling you do, you must have a minimum number of students. For example, if you wish to compare results from an experimental and a control group (two groups) in first and second grade (two grade levels), then you must do four matrix samplings. If you have 30 objectives, this means that you must have at least 30 students in each group, e.g., 30 second graders in the control group. For each matrix sample you construct, follow steps 2 through 7.

2. Determine the number of objectives or items to be covered by each test part. The maximum number you should attempt to cover is 10 objectives or 50 items per part. The number of objectives or items you decide to cover on each part will be determined by the ability of the students and the difficulty of the subject matter. Remember that this number affects the minimum number of students you will need for testing.

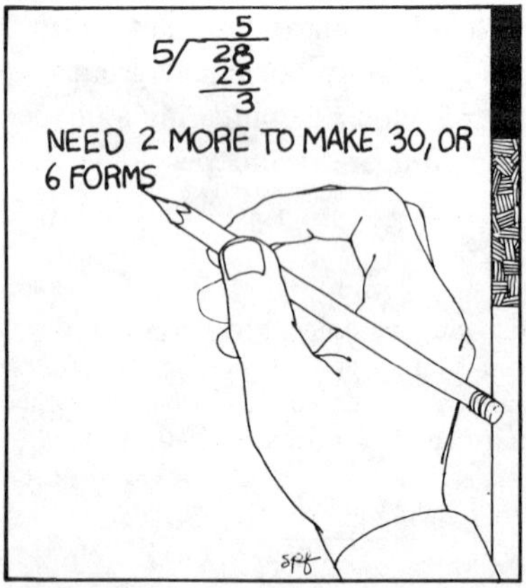

3. Divide the total number of objectives (or items) you have in all by the number you plan to include in each part. Quite obviously, this tells you how many test parts you will have. It also tells you into how many sets you will have to divide your students: one set to take each test part. If the total number of objectives or items is not evenly divisible by the number you have chosen per part, then fill in—randomly pick some objec-

tives or items from the larger pool to make up the difference. These few objectives or items will simply be tested more often than the others. For example, if you have a total of 28 objectives written on cards, and you wish to assign 5 objectives to each test part, then you will be two objectives short. Collect these two objectives by randomly pulling two cards from the pile. Make a duplicate of each of these cards, and add them to the pool.

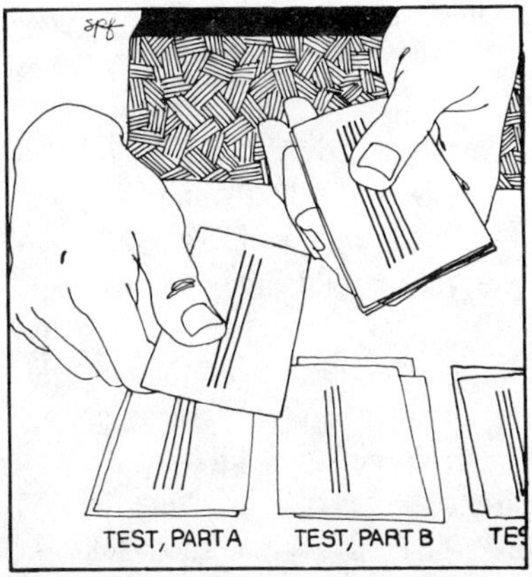

4. Randomly assign objectives (or items) to test parts. If they are already on cards, shuffle the cards thoroughly and deal them into piles, one pile for each test part. If they are included on a written list, number them and use a random-numbers table, a deck of numbered cards, or some other method for doing the randomization.

5. If you have been randomizing objectives, then collect or write items for each objective, and assign them to the proper test parts.

6. Give the items for each test to the typist with instructions to type each test part as though it were a separate test. Be sure to leave space for names and vital information at the top of the first page of each test part. Make sure all the pages of each part are securely stapled. Mark an unobtrusive letter ("A," "B") on the front page to identify each test part.

7. Randomly assign students to take the test parts. An adequate randomization of students to test parts can be done in either of these ways:

(a) Mix up the test booklets containing each of the test parts into a large stack: lay out the test parts in piles and mix them into blocks. For instance, if you have five test parts, then lay out parts A, B, C, D, and E on a table and mix them together in blocks of five. Place A, then B, then C, then D, then E onto the large pile, then repeat this placement over and over until you have placed them all into the large pile. At the time designated for testing, simply give out the test booklets from the large pile to the students. This will ensure that which student will get which part will be fairly randomly determined. Note that this procedure will have students within one classroom taking all the different test parts at the same time.

(b) If there is a reason for you to have all the students in a room take the *same* test part (perhaps to avoid the effects of children noticing that they have taken a different test), then you must randomly assign students to rooms for testing. To do this, assign a classroom to each test part, number a list of the students who will be tested, and use a random-numbers table, a deck of numbered cards, or some other method to assign students randomly to classrooms. Try to have the same number of students in each class.

Solution 4: Assigning Priorities Through Ratings–Retrospective Needs Assessment

A good way to keep testing to a minimum is to measure only the most important objectives. One way to identify the most important objectives is to have people rate them.

Determining a program's priorities through ratings is a technique often used when conducting a *needs assessment,* a statement of community or school objectives. Check to see if information from a previous needs assessment is available. If so, it may be possible to determine which goals and objectives the program's constituency prefers or what the intended emphasis of program planners has been. In the absence of this information, you can conduct a "Retrospective Needs Assessment" by choosing individuals from any of several groups who will be affected by the program (e.g., the original planners, teachers, students, parents, and community members) and having such individuals rate each program objective according to importance. Solution 4, although time-consuming for the evaluators and raters, yields evidence of the priorities of various interest groups and is recommended when the acceptance of the evaluation by divergent groups is a major concern. Step-by-step instructions for Solution 4 follow.

Instructions for assigning priorities to objectives through ratings. The evaluator can provide a focus for the evaluation by pursuing the following rating procedure.[11] The procedure can be used at a group meeting or through the mail.

1. Obtain a list of program objectives, or if you are authorized to do so, prepare a list yourself. Potential sources of objectives are listed in this booklet (see page 24). The objectives selected will be rated for importance by a panel of raters.

   There should be enough objectives to ensure adequate coverage, but not more than can be rated by one person (roughly, not more than 150). If there are too many objectives, they should be grouped into categories representing more general goals. If it is not feasible or desirable to make such combinations, prepare several overlapping sets of objectives so that raters rate subsets of the total pool of objectives.

   It is not necessary that objectives be expressed in behavioral form. Any of the formats described in Chapters 1 and 3 of this booklet are suitable. What is important is that raters have a precise understanding of what the objective is. Use whatever language will ensure such understanding in your situation. Make sure, though, that

11. Using this procedure provides your evaluation with a legitimate needs assessment. A needs assessment is an announcement of educational needs (as expressed in the school curriculum and in school policies) by representatives of the school or district constituency. The rating procedure described here is the most commonly used method for gathering community opinion about priorities placed on objectives. *It directs the rating of objectives from a previously prepared list.*

the objectives are all roughly equal in level of generality. Raters, it has been shown, will rate general objectives as more important than specific ones, regardless of their feelings about the relative importance of the actual subject matter.

2. Have the initial set of objectives reviewed separately by a few of the potential raters to verify comprehensiveness and clarity. Make sure that if parents and students are to be rating the objectives, extra care will be taken to ensure that the language used in both the objectives and the instructions is appropriate to their reading level and familiarity with the subject matter.
3. Print the final set of objectives on cards or slips of paper, one objective per card. Number each objective for ease in recording the ratings.

   Below appears an illustration of objectives for a science program.

```
No. 6

To be able to explain the idea of classification giving
examples from the Linnean system.
```

```
No. 63

To explain man's ecological relationship to animal and
plant organisms in his environment.
```

4. Prepare a set of five envelopes for each rater. These envelopes should be labeled as follows:

1 point	Unimportant, inappropriate, or irrelevant
2 points	Below average importance
3 points	Average importance
4 points	Above average importance
5 points	Very important, critical, or essential

5. Select raters. This is a critical step since the viewpoints of the raters will determine the final outcome. It is generally best to use various

kinds of raters, such as teachers, parents, students, school board members, curriculum experts and consultants, community pressure groups, principals, counselors, department heads, district administrators, etc. The type and number of raters from each category is a function of the size and importance of the task. For example, it is more important to involve the community in selecting goals for the district than in rating the objectives for a 5th-grade math course. On the other hand, the advice of math curriculum experts is more valuable in rating elementary math objectives than in rating goals for the district. Thus, when you select raters, consider the scope of opinions that you need and each rater's relevant expertise, involvement in setting up and running the program, and participation in the program.

In most cases, 10 to 15 raters should provide an adequate rating group. Remember that it is better to include too many people than to omit someone who should have been involved. In many instances, of course, it is not practical to include all concerned people as raters, such as all the parents of children in the school district. If you wish to limit the number of people involved, select a stratified random sample.[12]

Give the group of raters a composition that will proportionately represent different interest groups. If teachers and parents' views seem equally important, have the same number of teacher and parent raters. If program planners or curriculum experts' opinions seem more important, then include more planners than parents or teachers, or weigh each planner's responses accordingly (e.g., you might count each planner's ratings twice to accomplish this).

6. Call raters together for a meeting, or send them the rating materials through the mail. For convenience and for purposes of reaching consensus, a meeting is the better method. Carefully instruct raters about the rating procedure. Figure 2 presents a form letter describing a set of sample instructions. It may be possible to adapt these instructions to your situation.

---

12. This is a random sample which ensures that each important group is adequately represented. Directions for stratified sampling can be found in most texts on research design, or in the chapter on randomization in the book, *How to Design a Program Evaluation,* part of the *Program Evaluation Kit.*

Mountain Unified School District • Board of Education • 11 North Pine Rd. • Mountain, California 96177

October 28, 19xx

Dear (Parent, Student, Administrator, Teacher),

Thank you for agreeing to participate in ranking the goals of the Forge Ahead in Reading (FAIR) Program. Enclosed is a list of others who have also agreed to lend us their opinions.

As you know, we are currently in the process of evaluating FAIR for the School Board. The evaluation will look for ways in which the program can be improved or expanded. It will also likely have an effect on the amount of money allotted for the program in future years.

The Board wants this evaluation to obtain the best and most complete information possible about how well the FAIR Program has met the highest priority goals of the community regarding reading achievement. We already have a list of the project's goals. Our problem is to identify the *most important ones*. These will guide the evaluation.

You have been invited to help in this effort, which will tell us what deserves the most attention when we study FAIR's accomplishments. You have been specially selected as a representative of one or another group--teachers, students, parents, administrators.

Along with the accompanying pack of 68 cards, each one bearing an objective of the FAIR program, you will find five small rating envelopes. There is also a large brown stamped envelope for returning the materials to us. The objectives differ in importance, and the program should devote more time, effort, and resources to having the students achieve some of them than it should devote to others. Similarly, progress in achieving the more important goals should be monitored more closely to ensure early detection of problems.

When you make your ratings, think about the children that you know the best, and ask yourself: Among all that they should learn and be able to do, which of these are of the most value?

Figure 2. Sample letter instructing respondents about objectives rating procedure

Page Two
October 28, 19xx

Rating Procedure:

1. Place the five envelopes in front of you from left to right.

2. Look through the whole set of cards briefly to get an idea of the range of importance of the objectives. Try to think of objectives that *you* think are important which we might have overlooked. Write these on one of the blank cards provided. Now find one objective for each of the five categories of importance, and sort these cards on top of the corresponding envelopes.

3. Sort the remaining cards into these same piles. Be sure to put at least five cards in each pile and to place every card in some pile. If you are not sure into which pile a goal should be placed, put it into the one to which you feel it comes closest. Do not spend too much time deciding; if you have difficulty in rating a card, put it at the back of the pack and sort it last. There are no right or wrong answers in this task. Just rate the goals in terms of how important *you* think they are.

4. When you have sorted all the cards, check that you have put at least five cards in each pile. Put the cards into the corresponding envelope, and return all the materials to us. *On the brown envelope, please check the appropriate box indicating whether you are a parent, teacher, student, or administrator.*

Try to complete your task and return the objectives to us by November 5. If you have any questions, please feel free to call me at the Board of Education offices.

Sincerely,

Gerry Cooper

Gerry Cooper
FAIR Program Evaluator

GC:dc
Encls.

Figure 2. (continued)

7. Have the objectives rated for importance. Make sure each rater rates all the goals on the same scale of importance. Use a 5-point scale where you rate 5 = very important, 4 = above average importance, 3 = average importance, 2 = below average importance, and 1 = unimportant. Make a provision for goals that may have been overlooked while constructing the original set of goal cards by providing a few blank cards to each rater for write-ins.
8. Collect and record the rating data. Obtain the complete set of ratings from all the selected raters and accurately record the ratings for each objective.
9. Once the ratings are compiled, compute the average rating per objective. To do this, add up the *points* assigned to the objective by all the raters, find the *total* points assigned, and divide this by the number of raters. This will give you the *mean.* A good practice is to set up a roster for ratings such as the following:

Sample Roster of Ratings

Objective number	Raters (N=8) 1	2	3	4	5	6	7	8	Total	Mean (total÷8)
1	5	3	1	2	1	5	4	4	25	3.13
2	1	2	1	4	5	1	3	1	18	2.25
3	3	3	3	2	3	4	3	3	24	3.0

10. The mean ratings appearing on the roster are the end product of the rating process. Focus the evaluation on the objectives with the highest mean ratings—as many of them as you feel your resources can manage. If you note disagreement among raters which you cannot resolve yourself, consult the group again to negotiate differences.

If you find that your evaluation must answer the wishes of two (or more) different *interest groups* and that these groups emphasize different objectives for the program, alter steps 9 and 10:

9–alternate. Once the ratings are compiled, compute the average rating for the raters representing each interest group. Set up your ratings roster to show group differences.

Sample Roster of Ratings From Three Groups

Obj. No.	Teachers (N=3) 1	2	3	Total	Mean	Parents (N=4) 1	2	3	4	Total	Mean	Students (N=2) 1	2	Total	Mean
1	3	4	5	12	4.0	4	5	3	3	15	3.75	3	4	7	3.5
2	1	1	2	4	1.33	4	4	5	5	18	4.5	2	3	5	2.5
3	3	3	2	8	2.67	1	3	2	4	10	2.5	5	5	10	5.0
4	1	2	1	4	1.33	2	2	1	1	6	1.5	2	1	3	1.5
5	2	1	2	5	1.67	1	2	2	2	7	1.75	2	2	4	2.0

10–alternate. Again, objectives with the highest mean ratings will become the most important ones for your evaluation. In this case, however, focus on the top objectives *per group,* evaluating as many as your resources allow. In the sample roster above, objective 1 was rated highly by teachers, objective 2 by parents, and objective 3 by students. Such divergence of opinion, it should be noted, is more the exception than the rule.

Solution 5: Assigning Priorities Through Objectives Hierarchies

Solution 5 presents a different way to determine the importance of objectives. Here the objectives are logically ordered according to whether they describe simple, basic skills or complex, terminal skills. "Terminal" objectives should receive high priority, since they involve mastery and integration of lesser, prerequisite skills. This method is useful when the subject matter has a clearly discernible logical structure and therefore lends itself to hierarchical arrangements.

The construction of hierarchies has the advantage of requiring just one or two people–the evaluator, and possibly a consultant–to determine program priorities. Procedures for constructing objectives hierarchies grew out of the work of educational psychologists concerned with task analysis in the mid-60's. Task analysis is a method by which a complex skill, such as doing long division or repairing the transmission on an automobile, is analyzed into a series of simpler skills.

Hierarchies, or charts of prerequisites, are used in task analysis to show the relationships among the component skills that are thought to comprise a complex skill. Long division, for instance, is dependent on the ability to multiply, to subtract, to find the greatest multiple of the divisor that is not more than the dividend, and so forth. Each of these skills, in turn, is dependent on other prerequisite skills. Finding the desired multiple of the divisor depends on a good working knowledge of the multiplication tables; and multiplication, in turn, depends on simpler skills like addition, being able to read and write numerals, being able to keep track of one's place when reading a series of digits, and so on to even simpler sensory-motor skills. A hierarchy of skills is the result of such an analysis of skills into simpler and simpler components.

Figure 3 shows a partial skill hierarchy for long division. Notice that as

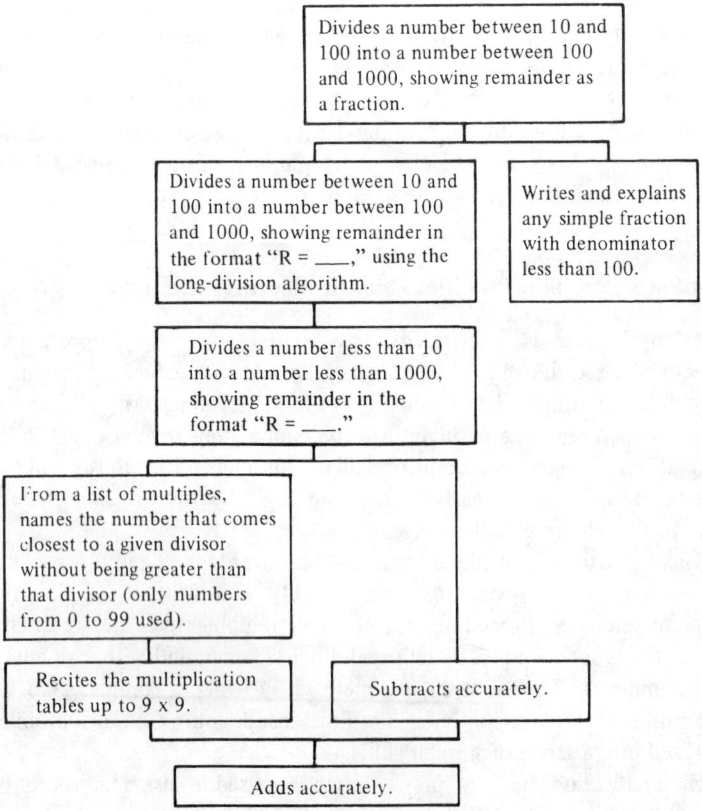

Figure 3. Portion of long division skill hierarchy

you read from the bottom of the chart to the top, the skills become increasingly complex, building on the simpler ones. Note also that sometimes simpler skills feed into more than one complex skill.

A hierarchy can be thought of as the map of a pipeline of learning, flowing from the bottom to the top. Before skills of the higher levels can be learned, learning must pass through the lower valves. These lower skills are necessary prerequisites for the higher, later ones. Each higher-order skill subsumes, or includes as part of itself, the lower-level skills that have come before. Task analysis charts like Figure 3 are generally used in curriculum design. They pinpoint the skills necessary to be taught, and they outline the *sequence* in which skill teaching should probably occur.

If you will be working with already written objectives, your hierarchy construction will not need to involve the amount of work that task analysis obviously does. You will not have to start from scratch, analyzing tasks. You have the components already provided in the form of objectives. The task of constructing a hierarchy from written objectives involves arranging the objectives according to their relationship to each other, much like a pipeline chart.

Following are some step-by-step instructions for constructing an objectives hierarchy for already written objectives.

Instructions for assigning priorities to objectives through hierarchies

1. Collect all the objectives for the program. Since you will be arranging objectives according to their interrelationships, either have them typed on small index cards, or list them on a piece of paper and cut the paper into strips with one objective on each.

2. Group objectives together according to subject matter and topic area. Make piles of objectives according to topic area and try to give a general name to each, e.g., sensory-motor skills, reading comprehension, pre-algebra. How many groups you will have and the titles of these groups will depend entirely on the nature of your program. A program aimed at one subject (reading or math) will allow for fewer topic areas among objectives than will a broad program, such as one that covers a whole primary grades curriculum. A good rule-of-thumb is to try to keep to fewer than 10 topic areas.

3. Construct a hierarchy chart for each group of objectives. Use a large piece of wrapping paper or a blackboard. You might use a blank wall or a large table top, though these might not be suitable for drawing connecting lines among objectives. Divide the sheet or board into three equal sections by drawing two horizontal lines across it. You will need one of these divided sheets for each topic group.

4. Begin your hierarchy by classifying each of the objectives in the group as *basic, intermediate,* or *complex*. Place them (masking tape works best) in the bottom, middle, or top third of the chart respectively. A *basic* objective will measure a skill that is important to the learning of some, but not necessarily all, of the others, and is built on skills so fundamental that they are not included as a focus of the program.

Intermediate objectives describe skills that are built from the basic ones and in turn are components of the complex ones. *Complex* objectives will tend to be built upon the basic and intermediate objectives. Some objectives will not neatly fit into the scheme of interrelationships; while dealing with the same general topic area, they will not seem to be built upon nor precede any of the others. In such cases, decide whether the particular objective is basic, intermediate, or complex in terms of skills for children of the age in question and its relationship to skills not included in the program's objectives. Then place the objective on the chart, omitting connecting lines.

5. Build the hierarchy. Arrange basic objectives under the intermediate ones into which they "feed." Then do the same for the complex ones. Draw lines of connection among objectives that are related. When two objectives feed into or are fed by a single objective, use branching lines to show this.

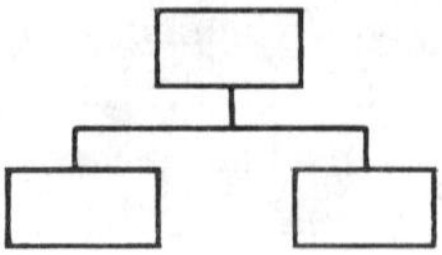

For example, if two basic objectives feed into a more complex objective, show it in this way.

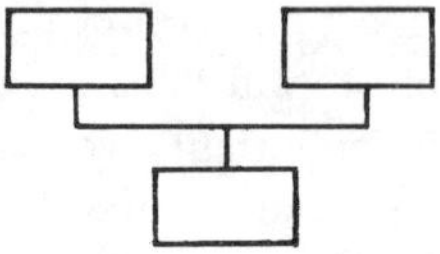

Likewise, if one basic objective is a prerequisite for two more advanced objectives, show it like this.

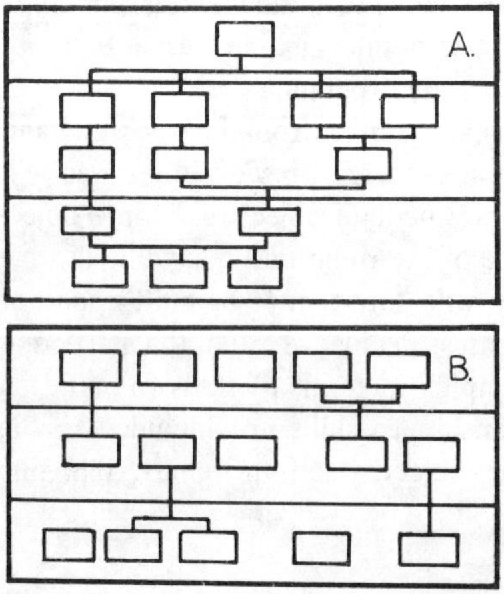

Some topic areas will turn out to be composed of objectives that are closely interrelated; each objective will share myriad connections with the others. Other topic areas will show only sparse interrelatedness among objectives. Either case will be useful to you. The drawing illustrates the sorts of hierarchy charts produced by great interrelation (A) or lack of interrelation (B) in the topic area.

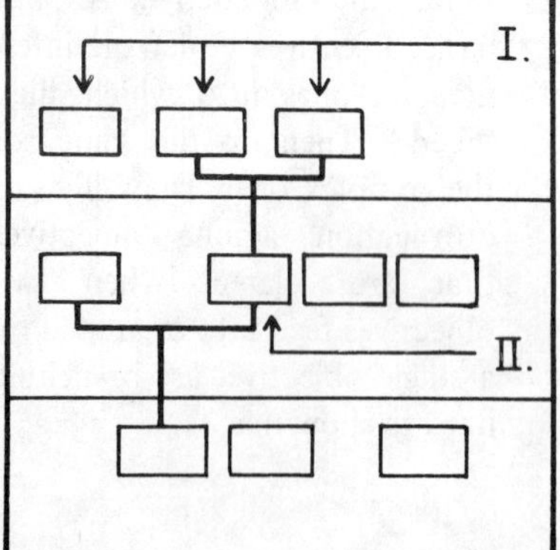

6. Choose the objectives to which you will give priority.

a. Objectives at the top of an interconnected string should be assessed. These are the *terminal* or top objectives, the ultimate goals of the program. Objectives that have been judged complex, but which do not have intermediate and/or basic objectives feeding into them, should also be considered terminal objectives. These are the objectives (labeled "I" in the accompanying diagram) to which your evaluation should address itself.

b. Find the key intermediate objectives from which the hierarchy branches upwards (labeled "II" in the diagram). These objectives can be considered crucial to mastery of higher ones and therefore important for the program to accomplish.

c. If possible, assess objectives that you considered intermediate in your initial sorting, but which did not, in the end, lead to any more complex ones.

d. If you can (that is, if you have time and opportunity), assess some of the lesser objectives also.

The above procedure should provide you with an objectives hierarchy that will be adequate to focus the efforts of your evaluation on the most important program goals.

A word should be said here about omissions. The procedure described here usually leads the hierarchy builder to discover omissions in the statement of program objectives. It may become apparent, for example, that one of the complex objectives could be facilitated by the inclusion of a more basic objective that was left out or taken for granted.

For Further Reading

On matrix sampling . . .

Husck, T. R., & Sirotnik, K. Matrix sampling. *Evaluation Comment,* 1968, *1*(3). (UCLA Center for the Study of Evaluation).

Sirotnik, K. Introduction to matrix sampling for the practitioner. In W. J. Popham (Ed.), *Evaluation in education: Current applications.* Berkeley: McCutchan Publishing Co., 1974.

On objectives hierarchies . . .

Davies, I. K. *Competency-based learning: Technology, management, and design.* Chapter 3: Analyzing the task. New York: McGraw-Hill, 1973.

Gagne, R. M. *The conditions of learning.* New York: Holt, Rinehart & Winston, 1970.

Index